Network Marketing
Is Not A <u>Bad Word</u>.

A Different Perspective About
Your Great Home Business.

Zuberi Olushola

zuberiwoods@netscape.net

Copyright 2014

TABLE OF CONTENTS

Introduction

Network Marketing is a wonderful and unique business concept and totally different way to earn money. It gives the average individual the chance to achieve two things that most cannot get with a job; <u>Financial Freedom</u> and <u>Time Freedom</u>. Not only from your efforts but also from the efforts of others. Imagine the real possibility of living the life of your dreams by having a part-time home business and earning a monthly residual income that could exceed your present job salary.

Unfortunately, for too long this business model has been misunderstood and sometimes not clearly explained. Many people are missing out on a wonderful financial opportunity. This is a simple business. Simple, yet challenging because you are in the people business. <u>Once a month</u>, independent reps are asked to do one thing, buy products. When a new rep joins the company thru your team and buy products once a month, you get paid. You have contributed to bringing more customers to the company as independent reps and you are being rewarded for your efforts in the form of a cash payment. When you look at some of the top money earners in this business, simply, what they have is a very large team of independent reps. Individuals who each order company products once-a-month.

The misinformed think that it is impossible to earn $2000, $5000, $10,000, $20,000 or more a month and not have a legitimate job or be an entertainer or athlete. Network Marketing is a home business where it is absolutely possible and people are doing it every day.

Why start a home business?

- ☐ More family time
- ☐ Low start up cost.
- ☐ You are the boss.
- ☐ Make as much or little money as you want.
- ☐ Flexible schedule.
- ☐ Work it part time.
- ☐ Tax benefits.
- ☐ Low risk/high reward.
- ☐ Very low overhead.

In these challenging economic times, it is unfortunate that many people are missing out on such a great financial opportunity because of the long held misconceptions about this business.

It is difficult for people to believe in something that they do not clearly understand. Network Marketing Representatives along with the Network Marketing companies must do more to change the image of this business by better educating prospects.

<u>It does not matter how great a business is OR how much money someone can make. If your prospects do not believe that the "method" you are using to make money is legitimate, they will not join you.</u>

This is the disconnect and a big reason why some reps do not succeed in this business.

It is not that Network Marketing doesn't work. It's the way that it is being explained or introduced that does not work. "Network Marketing Is Not A Bad Word", was written so that you, the Independent Rep. can better understand and explain the Network Marketing Concept. It will empower you to operate from the position of a <u>business owner</u> more so, than an independent representative. It removes the need for slick words and methods to get people to join your team. It is critical for you to first understand this business model before you talk to prospects about products or company. You will be able to stay focused on how to use your time and energy. This is important as it is very easy to do things that have nothing to do with building your home business.

You will not read a lot about product selling here. All companies in the industry claim to have the best, most nutritional, miracle curing products. This book was not written to talk about the nutritional value of products but to show you the financial benefits of Network Marketing. Understanding the Network Marketing Concept is very important.

You want to become grounded to the point where you are proud to say that you are a part of this industry. There is absolutely no need to lie or be ashamed. Start your career off right by being honest with your prospects about your home business.

Network Marketing is a low risk, high reward business model that can be used to obtain a wonderful lifestyle for you and your loved ones. It is low risk because of the low joining fee. If you ever decide to terminate your distributorship, call the company and request to do so. It is that simple.

You have to put your 9 to 5 mindset on hold and be open to learn about a new way to earn money.

Whether you are new to Network Marketing, thinking about joining or have been in business for awhile, "Network Marketing Is Not A Bad Word" will give you a totally new perspective and focus for success with your home business. This is your own unique, journey to the top!

Note: It is recommended that this book is read more than once to help you better internalize the information. Several words will be used interchangeably in this book.

Independent Representative, Business Owner, Customer, Rep, Team Member all have similar meanings.

A Little About Me.

I first heard about Network Marketing in my early twenties. An older lady and her friend invited me and my friend, Curtis to their meeting one evening. The company was A. L. Williams. They were excited about attending. We politely declined. It was one of those "Pyramid things" we said.

A few years later, a good friend of ours called. He said that he was having a "party" and we were invited. When we got there, it was an opportunity meeting for Amway. We left mad and disappointed that we had been tricked in coming to a 'Pyramid Scheme" instead of a party.

Just a few years ago, a guy gave me his business card. His name was on the front along with a picture of a bottle of juice. He asked me to take a look at his website. When I did, I saw the same bottle of juice. "Another pyramid", I thought.

A few weeks later, I heard about a business opportunity meeting and stopped by to listen in. A young lady was giving the presentation. Her name was Diane. She spoke about her company, the products and how to start a home business as a way to make money. She got my attention when she explained how you get paid not only from your efforts but also by incorporating the efforts of others.

This was the same company as the one on the card that the guy had given to me. I signed up the next week and started on my Network Marketing journey.

Do you remember the distributor that hit the top company position in record time? Well, that wasn't me. Or the Triple-Diamond-Jade-Gold Executive? That wasn't me either. How about the person who won all of the exotic trips, bonuses, cash and cars? Nope, not me. I was the "getting ready to-get- ready" guy. The one that went to all of the company meetings, Super Saturdays, on every conference call but wasn't getting any checks. (Sounds familiar?)

Oh, I did have some success with sponsoring prospects but nowhere near what I had envisioned.

What was my problem? I did (almost) everything that I was "trained" to do. So, why was I not getting better results?

I did not realize at the time that many of the methods for sponsoring prospects did not work for me personally. I also learned that my efforts and focus (no matter how sincere) were very misplaced. I was spending too much time doing things there were benefiting my up line and company, but was doing very little for my personal home business success. Although my personal success had not come, two things made sense to me:

1. Network Marketing is a legitimate profession and great business model that can give you the financial freedom that you desire.
2. Residual Income is a great income stream and way to have more time freedom.

I came to realized that I was the missing piece to this equation. In order for me to succeed and help others, I had to become more educated about the

MLM (Multi Level Marketing) business.

I did not quit on myself or learning about this industry. I continued to attend conference calls, study other leaders and successful people, read books, watch videos, and listened to CD's. I continued on my personal journey to become a more, well rounded person who can help others know more about this great industry.

"Network Marketing Is Not A Bad Word" was written based on my own experiences, research and observations of successful money earners in Network Marketing. It is my purpose to help people from the very beginning to better understand the Network Marketing business model, and where to keep their energy and focus. To your success!

Mindset: Never, Ever Quit.

First things, first. Never quit your business. When you step into the world of Network Marketing, you must be open to accept that there are other ways to earn money. Getting paid over here is totally different than how you get paid at your job. You must be able to put your 9 to 5 mentality to the side and accept that there are unconventional ways to earn a living. People do it every day. Think about how actors, artists, athletes and entertainers get paid. There are many, many ways to earn money and Network Marketing is one of them.

The 2 main questions that many people ask themselves when joining this business is, "Can I do this? "or "Will this work for me?" The answer is, absolutely! If you never quit. Quitting is your only failure. Just understand that every meeting, conference call, local, regional or national event is a part of your training. Every time someone tells you "no" or does not show up when they said that they would, you are in training. Every conversation with a prospect or rep from another company is training. So, there is no failure unless you quit.

I was recently talking with my good friend, Corey. He was an independent rep with another Network Marketing company. I asked him how his business was going. He said that he was not doing anything now which meant that he had quit his business.

He like so many others did not understand that just because he had not yet met his goals, meant that he had failed. He had been in this business for less than a year. All situations are a part of your training and process toward your journey to success, so never quit. Get it?

As you face new challenges in your Network Marketing career, it is critical for you to develop a mindset that will empower you to conquer obstacles and challenges. Anyone can succeed in Network Marketing yet, it is not for everyone.

Becoming a success in this business depends on many factors. The main factor is you. It all starts with your goals, desire and beliefs. These are areas in which you will need to be strong for success. How bad do you want this? Are you willing to go the distance despite the obstacles and disappointments that may come your way? Are you willing to sacrifice your time and energy to increase your value to others?

Personal development trainer and international speaker Jerry "DRhino" Clark calls it the "Rhino Mentality" in that you must develop "thick skin" in this business. T.O.P.G.U.N. Founder and top producing, Network Marketing Multimillionaire, Robert Dean Jr. calls it that, "burning desire" and Motivational Speaking Icon, Les Brown says, "You have to be hungry!" to reach your goals and dreams. This mentality takes time for many to develop. With others, it is already there. One of the biggest mistakes many individuals make upon joining this industry is that they give up much too soon. As soon as a challenge or obstacle appears, they assume that Network Marketing is a scam, get scared and quit.

They did not have overnight success or yet understand that there will be challenges along their journey. In this business just like in life, you will succeed if you do not quit. As motivational speaker, Anthony "Tony" Robinson says, "There are no failures, only results."

Once you have a better understanding about what you should do and where to keep your focus, you will develop a "no quit" mindset when challenges show up. You will conquer them, stay focused and keep moving forward. This book will give simple explanations about your role, your company's role and your relationship between the two.

It is said that a 1,000 mile journey begins with the first step. As with any new endeavor, there is a learning curve. Your career in Network Marketing is no different. There are no short cuts. The key here is to develop a <u>never quit</u> mindset.

This is critical, because once you clearly understand the Network Marketing business model and concept, you will then grow more confident in your ability to share it with others and succeed in this business. Your focus, energy and commitment will get stronger and you will not get shaky or quit when challenges appear and attempt to derail your business. There is a saying, "You will be bad before you are good, and good before you are great". This is a process and not get rich quick. You must crawl before you walk. It is important to understand that the strategy or method that your up-line used may not work for you. If it does not work for you right away doesn't mean that you are a failure. Find out what adjustments you personally need to make and keep going. Many people spend months or years in this business doing things that they were taught, only to later realize that it did not work for them. This is not a reason to quit!

I recall watching basketball great, Michael Jordan play in a game against the New York Knicks. He had the ball and attempted to drive to the basket along the baseline. Knicks center, Patrick Ewing had his path blocked. Jordan reversed back toward the sideline, then came back along the baseline toward the basket and dunked over two players! If he could not make it to the basket one way, he would try another and another. Most ball players would have stopped after the first or second attempt but, MJ did not stop until he reached the goal and put the basketball into the hoop. His focus, determination and no quit attitude made him the best in the world. That is how you must be with your business, focused and committed. You pull back, regroup and go again. Find out what does work for you based on your experiences along with your style, and personality. Your road to success may have a different path than your up line or sideline. It may not come as fast or may come faster. Many people tell their own stories of how success came differently than they expected.

Actor, Will Smith first started out as a rap artist. While he did have success in music, he is more famous today for being one of the best actors in the world. Michael Jordan's dream was to be a professional baseball player. His success came in basketball. Your road to success may not be straight. It may have many different twists, turns and a few roadblocks. This is a part of the journey. Talk with successful leaders in this business and they will share their stories with you. Understand that success is yours and waiting for you to come to it. The secret is to never quit!

This is the key to your success. <u>You might change companies, but never, ever quit your business</u>!

This is A Partnership.

When you pay your fee and join a new company, you have entered into a partnership (agreement) between you and the company. It is a business relationship, period. It is fun to go to the conventions, local meetings and fall in love with the company and new products. It is still a business relationship.

In this partnership between the new rep and the company, each party agrees to fulfill their monthly agreements. You, as a representative or distributor, agrees to purchase via auto shipment a certain amount of products each month from the company. In return, the company will send you their products. Basically, the company is using you as a "vehicle" to move their products and build their brand. You are using the company as a "vehicle" to reach your goals. Remember! This is a partnership.

When someone joins your team and order products (via auto-ship) as you do, you will be paid. As your team grows, your title and money grows, again and again. You also position yourself to receive additional bonuses and prizes as you help others on your team succeed.

You are an "Independent Representative." No matter what Network Marketing company you join, and no matter what title you are given, there is always a particular word that is attached to your title. It does not matter if you are a consultant, Rep, Distributor etc. The one word that always precedes your title is the word, INDEPENDENT. Why? Because, as an independent representative, you are on your own. You are not an employee of the company. You do not get paid by the hour. There is no sick time or health benefits and surely no one will call you about coming to work. Yes, you are an "independent" representative for the company. You are also the boss, team-leader, up-line support and CEO of your own home business.

As a business owner, you must always work in the interest of your home business first. Let the company take care of company business. Which is to promote and sell THEIR products. You promote your home business opportunity. <u>Take care of your home business and the company will take care of you.</u>

You have no boss because you are the boss of your own home business. Your success lies in doing the things listed below consistently in the "Independent Rep" column.

Company	Independent Rep.
Create / Sell Products	Order/ Buy Products
Promote Company/ Products	Promote Opportunity/Company/Products
Pay/Train Independent Distributors	Sponsor/ Build Team Support/ Train Team

This is just the first part of beginning to build an income from home. Companies each have their own specific compensation plan and qualification requirements, policies and rules.

I remember once attending a Network Marketing company's national convention in Las Vegas. It was a blast. I met distributors from many countries and got to meet the founders of the company. There was all kind of activities. I purchased every DVD, T-shirt, brochure and product that I could buy. The founders showed videos of their vision for the future of the company and gave away lots of money and prizes.

I fell in love. I pledged my allegiance to tell the world about "my" company. It was so one-sided on my part. I ordered the products, all of their material and promoted the company. I thought that by promoting the company and products, I would also be promoting my home business. It does, but not the way in which you may envision.

You can buy all of the banners, go to every meeting and get on every training call, but if you are not adding people to your team who are ordering products, you will not get a check.

I soon began to understand that the distributor-company relationship is a business relationship. Period. When you purchase their products and bring them more distributors, you will get paid. No production, no cash.

That is the business and how it should be. It is not about friendship, it's about business. Your company's loyalty goes as far as your next purchase or sign-up. Your loyalty should be based on whether your company can help you reach the goals that you have set.

I have not met anyone who ever received a check for listening to a conference call, going to a meeting or wearing a nice suit or dress. You will not be paid just because you have the company's brochures, posters and car magnets. This is a business partnership. When you buy products and build a productive team, you will be paid accordingly. This is a partnership, not a job.

In most cases, when working a job, you will be paid for showing up and sticking around for 8 hours a day/40 hours a week. You may do a little work, play some solitaire on the computer, take a few smoking breaks, not be very productive and still get a check. In Network Marketing, your pay is based solely on productivity and results. This simply means that you order your products once-month, build a team and help them to do the same. No new people, no product movement, no checks. Period.

Selling Is Optional.

Retail Sales is offered as one of several ways that you can make money in Network Marketing. As a rep, you purchase products at wholesale. Once you have made your monthly purchase from your company, the products are yours to do as you choose. You can consume them or give them away. You can also sell them at a higher price to recoup your initial cost plus a small profit. That is your option. The company will not call you to see if you have sold your products. Why? Because once you have made your monthly purchase as an independent distributor, you have satisfied your part of the agreement with them. They have their money and you have your products. They do not call you about selling your products or to order more products.

I stated earlier that selling is not required in order to make money. This is true. It is recommended by most companies but not required.

As an independent rep, you may decide to sell some products when you first join. However, you do not want to make this the main focus of your business.

You are new, excited and want to experience some feeling of success with your new business. Retailing your products are one of the quickest way to do this. That is understandable. However, do not become a product seller and delivery person. If you have some on hand, that is fine. Otherwise, send customers to your website.

Here is the problem with selling products for many distributors and why they eventually quit.
When you first get started in this business, you are new and your belief system is low. You are not sure if this Network Marketing thing really works. You are moving on faith and hope. Your support team has advised you to talk to friends and relatives about your business. You are told to do this by introducing the products to them. They may buy your products but, say "NO" to looking at the business opportunity. It becomes discouraging after a while to keep hearing NO, NO, NO from people that you just knew would jump into this business with you. They, like you, do not know or quite yet understand how this

Network Marketing thing works.

You then decide to just sell your products to avoid being told NO again. You make a few quick dollars. It feels good. You begin to feel like you are having some success and are on your way. It definitely feels better than being told NO.

After awhile, selling products gets old. Fewer people are buying your products and you are not making the money that you were told you could make. Soon, you begin wondering if this business is worth the money that you are putting in every month. You talk to fewer people. You get on fewer training calls. Your next move is to quit your business. This scenario happens many times. It is not because Network Marketing does not work. It clearly does. You are just focused on the wrong things.

Many reps spend most of their time focused on selling products rather than working to build a team of reps who order their products once a month and show others how to do the same.

If you spend most of your time in "selling mode" rather

than "team building mode", you will not stay in this business very long.

You joined your company because you want long term, big money. Retail selling is quick, temporary and unstable money. You have to keep finding new product customers and this can be tiresome. Plus, this will not get you residual income or time freedom.

It works for the company because selling is the company's main business. Your main business is people and opportunity. It costs less for the company to send you a rebate check instead of a residual check. Makes sense? This is not an anti-product or anti-company comment. The point is to make you aware of where to keep your focus and energy.

Which scenario makes more sense? You buying and trying to sell 100 cases of product per month OR having 100 people on your team who each order 1case of product per month?

In which case will you make the most money with the least effort? The second way of course.

As a business owner, focus your time on talking to people about the "opportunity" of Time & Financial Freedom and building a team. Stay focused and committed. In Network Marketing, you cannot "sell" your way to the top. People are your main business, not selling products.

Keep in mind, when reselling products that you have purchased, you are just recycling money that you have already spent. It is not connected to a payment from the company. That transaction is between you and the person who you sold them to. You can qualify for a rebate check for purchasing more products.

Purchases made by customers from your website, counts toward your overall product volume for a given period.

The Business Model

"As an independent representative, you enter into a partnership where you agree to order products once-a-month from your company. In return, the company pays you when new reps join your team and buys products once-a-month. In a nutshell, that is what you do and how you get paid."

What is the definition of Network Marketing? Many independent representatives (successful or not) do not know. To be successful in your home business and as you introduce it to others, it is very important that you first understand and can clearly explain Network Marketing and how it works. This is the method that Network Marketing companies use to move their products.

According to Webster's dictionary, the definition of Network Marketing is: A business model based on companies distributing products and services through a network of independent representatives.

31

There are several ways that companies move their products:

1) <u>Wholesale/Retail</u> (Local Chains, Sam's Club etc.)

2) <u>Direct Sales</u> (Avon, Mary Kay, Tupperware etc.)

3) <u>Network Marketing.</u>

Network Marketing AND Traditional companies (Coke, Frito-Lay, Oscar Mayer etc.) are <u>alike</u> because they want to accomplish two (2) things: <u>Sell their products and make money.</u>

Traditional and Direct Sales companies place their products in retail or big box stores.

They also spend millions of dollars in advertising costs on TV, radio, billboards etc.

<u>Network Marketing companies eliminate this middle step of the retail stores and do very little advertising.</u>

(This is one reason why the public at large knows so little about these companies and business model.)

<u>This accomplishes a couple of things:</u>

- It saves the company millions of dollars in advertising costs. They put this savings back into the company and products.

- And it gives them the ability to pay tremendous commissions and bonuses to their productive independent reps.

(<u>Note: Products made by Network Marketing companies are far better than similar products that you find in your local stores. They may cost more however; you get a higher quality product</u>.

Network Marketing companies sell their products directly to their Independent Representatives. The Independent Reps. arc also the <u>customers</u> for these companies. This is how products are moved and the companies stay in business. The advantage here is that as a customer/rep for the Network Marketing companies, you can also make money.

This is your primary responsibility as an independent rep; to be a customer to the company by purchasing their products on a monthly basis.

Now, what makes you want to return the next month and order more products?

Network Marketing companies offer incentives for you to continue your membership as a customer/independent rep. These companies want your business and will pay you very well when you bring them more business or new independent reps. You are paid when others join your team and order products each month from the company. You earn weekly and monthly income as new reps join your team via reps already on your team. Think of this as a <u>Referral Fee</u>.

One of the greatest aspects of this is business is that you can get paid on purchases by members on your team although you did not directly sponsor them. They can live near you, in another state or country. If they are somehow connected to your member I.D, their product purchases will count toward your overall team production which the company considers when determining the amount you will be paid for a given period.

Here is a basic example: You may receive payment on a percentage of your group's total product volume of 100 qualified reps although you only directly sponsored 5. By helping those 5 reps build their own teams, your team has grown to 100 reps. This is the beauty of the business. As your team grows, so will you income.

Traditional Companies	Network Marketing Companies
Products	Products
Spends money on advertising	Very little advertising. Spends money on product development and pay commissions to productive independent representatives.
Products go to retail outlets.	Bypass retail outlets. Products sold directly to representatives.
Customers purchase products.	Representative is customer.
Customers get coupons.	Customers get cash and bonuses.

Consider this: When you refer friends to a good restaurant, business or movie, the business may reward you with cash, a store credit or gift card.

Your friends enjoy the products or business and continue to patronize it. The company or business will continue to make money over and over, from your referrals but, not you. You will be paid <u>only once</u>.

As a Network Marketing Rep, you are paid weekly and monthly on your team purchases. Not just for your own personal efforts but also from the efforts of others on your team again and again.

This is how many individuals are able to fire their boss, travel and spend more time with family and loved ones.

Simply put, Network Marketing is another way for companies to move their products. Some use Retail/Wholesale, some use Direct Sales and some use the Network Marketing method.

The Network Marketing Concept:

What is Network Marketing?

A business model based on companies distributing their products through a network of independent distributors.

OBJECTIVES: To move their products and make money.

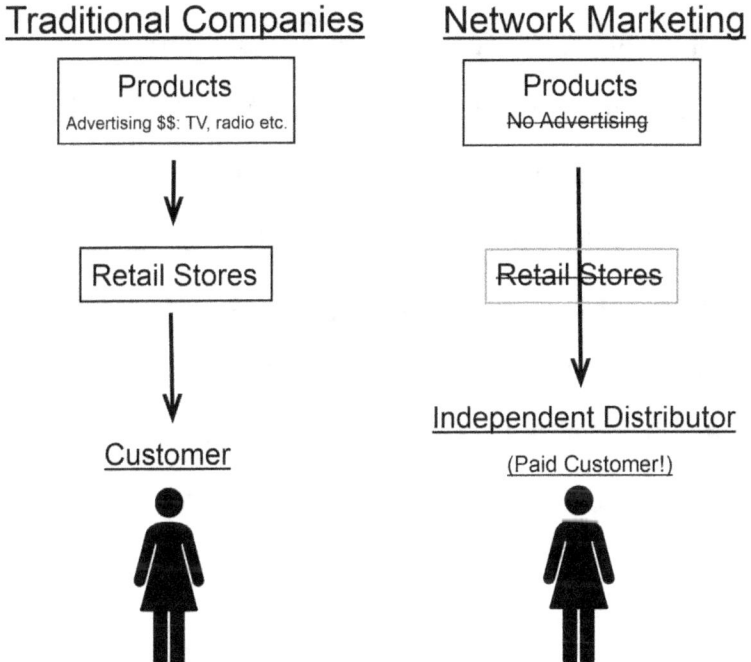

Traditional Companies	Network Marketing
Products — Advertising $$: TV, radio etc.	**Products** — ~~No Advertising~~
Retail Stores	~~Retail Stores~~
Customer	Independent Distributor (Paid Customer!)

All companies have different titles, compensation plans, products and incentives. You must decide which one best fits your goals. There are many great Network Marketing companies to partner with. With any company, do your homework. Find out about the stability of the company, its leadership and management team, compensation plan, products and quality of customer service.

What you should understand is that your earnings are not based on the <u>number</u> of people on your team but, on the amount of products that leaves the company's warehouse thru your team or organization via purchases. You may have 200 people in your group but few are participating, <u>qualified</u> reps. On the other hand, you may have only 100 qualified reps. who weekly or monthly product purchases are exceeding their requirements. Getting paid is about production, not people.

Opportunity-Company-Product.

Should you introduce the Opportunity, The Company or Products first?

As an "independent" representative, this is totally up to you. Your sponsor or support team may suggest that you show people your products and then the opportunity. When speaking to someone about your business, the <u>first</u> thing that you need to find out is if the person is even "looking" for an opportunity. This is important because you don't have time to waste trying to force someone to take a look at your business. If they are looking, find out what they want or desire and what has hindered them from achieving it so far. I have studied many leaders from different companies. What I have observed is that they made their money and built their teams by talking to prospects about Time Freedom, Financial Freedom and living their dreams. Not about how great a product may be.

This is the best way to start earning money. Some of my business partners just sold products and that is O.K.

They chose to build their business through their company's product and believed in it because of what it had done for them or a family member. They work alone and just want to make a few dollars to make ends meet.

In my experiences, when introducing the company's products to people first, you are often labeled as a product seller who is trying to recruit them to also sell products. That is a turn off to many and a big mistake many new distributors make. Leading with the product will get you labeled as a juice, vitamin or whatever "salesman". Introduce your business with the opportunity for <u>Financial and Time Freedom.</u> You explain how Network Marketing can be used as a vehicle to get them there.

A big reason for many reps. lack of success is because they are more focused on talking about their company's great, miracle curing products. Every company claims to have the greatest products and health benefits. But, that is the company's job. What will make you successful is educating people about Network Marketing, the company and then products, in that order. Your business is to educate people about the Network Marketing opportunity first.

When I came into this business, my team leader was "Product" oriented instead of "Opportunity" oriented. What I mean by this is that he liked to introduce people to Network Marketing by showing the products first. I sold some products but did not make much money. It became a hassle to deliver products. Many of my customers wanted a bigger discount than I could offer. I got into this business to make money, not to become a product seller.
Selling products gets you immediate, short term money, not residual income.

When you decide to lead with the opportunity, it is very important to be consistent with that introduction with your prospects. Opportunity, company, then products, in that order.

As I stated earlier, reps must do a better job of explaining the Network marketing concept before speaking about the products or company. The products may be great, but if your prospects do not believe in or understand the process of your business, they will be reluctant to join you.

Remember, you are an "independent representative". This is your business and you can run it anyway that you choose. Find out what works best for you. The most successful people that I know have built a successful business by leading with the business opportunity rather than product because it maximizes their time. <u>This means that more products are moved thru a team instead of just by you.</u>

If you have a product that has helped to improve people's health, then by all means, get it to them or have them order it from your website. Just do not make it the main focus of your business. People are not always looking for a new product to try. However, they are always looking for ways to have more money (Financial Freedom), and time (Time Freedom) to do the things that they desire. Show them how to use your business opportunity as a vehicle to get there!

Oh No!

Never did such a small word have so much power. It will break the spirit of many individuals who get into this business.

The word, "No" is a part of this business. Just accept it now and get ready to receive your share. Hearing it won't be personal but it will seem that way. Your ego will take some hits. Your pride will too. That's OK. It is a part of this business.

People hear this word in many ways every day. It just seems to have more power when you hear it in Network Marketing. Keep in mind that many people do not understand this business and think that it is not legitimate. They assume or have heard that it is a scam, usually from someone who has never been involved in this business, or stayed in for a very short period, then quit.

When you first get started, being told 'NO" just a few times will feel like having been hit by a large bolder. It seems to carry that much power to some. It bothers you because many of the people who say no are usually close to you. It seems personal. Many times, it is not. They are saying no to your Network Marketing business for now.

Hearing it is painful because your belief and understanding in what you are doing is low. You are not sure that this "pyramid" thing works either. The good news is that as your belief in this business grows, the power in that small, two letter word will shrink. Hearing "no" will then roll off of your shoulder like a small pebble.

Once you realize the power in what you have with this business and how it can change your life in ways you never imagined, you will then understand that when they tell you "no", it is their loss, not yours.

Be thankful when people tell you no. Their honesty saves you valuable time as opposed to someone that says "yes" and lead you on. Many times, you can turn a no into a "yes" by asking the right questions and giving clear explanations about your business. Many people are looking for a way to make some extra money. When you explain how Network Marketing is a legitimate business model and can get them what they are looking for, you can turn a no into a Yes! Begin by asking the right questions.

Setting Up For Success.

Getting organized and started on the right foot is important to your success. Your sponsor and support team will be there to assist you. If your sponsor lives in another city or state, it may be more challenging. However, you can still get started right with assistance via conference calls, webinar, DVD's etc.

As a Network Marketing Representative, you have many titles.

From the <u>company side</u>, you are:

1) Customer.

2) A independent distributor or representative.

3) Company representative.

Each company has different titles for their distributors. There are many more than those listed here. No matter the title, you are primarily a customer for the company.

From <u>your side </u>you are:

1) A home business owner.

2) Your own boss.

3) Team Leader/Support

Always, work first as a business owner which means organizing and preparing to build a large "productive" team.

For one day out of the month, you are asked to order products. Only one day. The company will not call or harass you. You are not forced to sell anything. You are not asked to buy extra products. You are only asked to buy at least the minimum amount of products each month to stay a "qualified representative". This is part of your partnership and agreement.

In this time, as a home business owner, you are learning more about the Network Marketing Concept and your company. You need to become familiar with all aspects of your company so that you can answer prospect's questions intelligently and with confidence. During this time, you want to begin to do the following:

☐ Learn about the company and become familiar with:

1. It's history.
2. It's Policies.
3. Training call times.

4. Compensation plan.

5. What it takes to advance to the next ranked position.

6. Products information.

7. Community involvement.

8. Quality of customer service. You want to know that the company can resolve your concerns, questions and problems with respect and in a timely manner.

☐ <u>Create a prospect list with the help of your sponsor and support team.</u> This will be a list of people that you want to contact and see if they are interested in learning more about your home business. Family, friends, co-workers, neighbors, church members etc.

Don't overlook anyone or take for granted that a certain person will not be interested. Give them a chance to say no.

With the help of your sponsor, you want to start speaking to individuals and find out if they are looking for a business opportunity. When first speaking to people, you only want to know if they are interested. <u>Do not try to</u>

give a presentation on the spot. <u>Save that for later in a better setting.</u>

Where do you find these people? You can start with people that you know and go from there. You will hear terms like Warm and Cold Market. Warm Market are people that you know, Cold Market are people that you don't know. It is natural to talk with people that you know first. You then talk with others. However, You don't have to limit yourself to warm and cold. You interact with hundreds of people every day. All are potential business partners. Remember, you need only a few to get started.

When calling, If you are not yet comfortable with explaining your business to prospects, set up a time with your support team member to assist you in inviting them to your event.

They can be there with you or in another location. Sometimes, when calling prospects, they want you to tell them everything over the phone. <u>Avoid doing this</u>. Keep it professional. Let them know that you are new to this business. However, your business partner can give them more information. Place them on hold while you place a **3-Way Call** to your support person. This is a valuable resource to use until you are comfortable calling and inviting on your own. It takes the pressure off of you and adds credibility to your business when a more experienced, knowledgeable person can assist you.

As you begin to speak to individuals, it is important to not waste your time. You want to ask questions that will let you know right away if that person is even looking for an opportunity. Your want to ask direct, specific questions that will get you an immediate answer. You also want to choose questions that are comfortable for you and not just the ones your sponsor tells you to use. You can modify questions to fit your style and comfort level when speaking to prospects. There are many different ways to ask questions to prospects. The point is to find out quickly if someone is hungry for something more than they have. You do not want to waste your time. Questions that may work for your up line, may not fit you. Below are a few sample questions:

1. "What do you think of Network Marketing?"
2. "What do you <u>know</u> about Network Marketing?"
3. "Have you taken a serious look at Network Marketing?
4. "Do you look for other ways to make money besides a job?"
5. "Would you be open to looking at a home business presentation?"
6. Have you ever been involved with Network Marketing?
7. What are your goals and dreams?

Your objective is to put as many prospects as possible in front of some type of presentation. It can be in person, over the phone, a webinar, CD or DVD.

Putting people in front of a presentation is the name of the game. This is how people come to know more about you, your company and your team.

Next, set up your In-home presentation with your support team for the prospects that are interested. They will do the presentation for you until you are ready to do them yourself. Some guests will come and some will not. Stay focused on the ones that kept their word and came. Don't dwell on the ones that did not.

During the presentation, your support person will explain the Network Marketing concept, your company information, and a brief description of the products, the compensation plan and how they can get started. Afterward, get with your prospects to see if they are ready to get started, have any questions or are not interested. They may want to buy some products.

If they are ready to get started, sign them up on your web site, the company phone or with a paper copy agreement. Help them set up their own home presentations. (List, calls, meetings etc.).

For the ones that can't make it to your home meeting. You can schedule a:

- 1-on-1 presentation (You and your prospect)
- 2-on-1(You, your sponsor and your prospect)
- A phone presentation.

- Webinar

- CD or DVD presentation.

There are many ways to present your opportunity. Showing some type of presentation is the key.

Let's be clear, this business is not for everyone yet, anyone can do it. Understand that everyone is not going to join your home business. It is not your responsibility to "convince" people to join your team. It is your responsibility find people who are looking and put them in front of some type of presentation. Your prospects will decide for themselves if they want to join your team.

A big mistake some reps make after giving a presentation, is they will stop prospecting and wait around for prospects to make a decision about joining. Do not do this!

The purpose of a presentation is to give information about the opportunity and company. It is not for you to sign someone up on the spot unless they are ready to do so.

Give the presentation, and move on to do the next

presentation. You want to give as many as possible. It is in the number of presentations given that you will find those who are looking for what you have.

After you have shown a presentation, you have done your part. Keep moving and find new prospects. You always want to add new names to your list.

There is a saying, "Some will, some won't, so what? Next!" This may sound harsh but it is the mindset you must have. Focus only on the yes's and not the no's. Keep repeating these steps until it becomes a part of you. There are thousands of people around you. Those first few can grow to many.

I remember one leader who had thousands of people in his organization. He had personally sponsored less than 25. That number grew and today he is a multimillionaire. You are just looking for a few serious individuals to get started with but, you should always look for new team members.

Some who join your team may not do anything. They may just want to order products and not build a team.

Personal sponsorship is an important part of your business if you choose to earn money. It is also a requirement by most legitimate companies that you personally sponsor a certain number of people in order to become a "qualified" representative. This means that you are now positioning yourself to begin earning commissions on future reps as your team begins to grow. Your team growth is not bound by geography. Another great aspect of this business is that you will receive credit for team members in any city, state or country that your company does business in.

As a sponsor, you want to assist your new business partners to become leaders of their own teams. You teach them what you have learned and are now doing. Your success lies in your team's success. When they are successful and reach new levels, so will you. In this business, you cannot be selfish. You must help others. Your ability to reach your goals and dreams is directly connected to helping others on your team reach theirs.

It is also important to understand that you are their

business partner and <u>not their boss</u>. Remember, you are an "independent" representative which means you have no boss. You help the ones that want help. You train and assist the members that have shown you that they are serious about building their business and team. You will know the ones who are serious because they are on the training calls and webinar before you are. They have made their list, set up their home meeting (presentation) and asked for your assistance. They ask questions, are open to learning something new and are coach-able.

Network Marketing is a simple business concept. Not always easy, but a simple one. It is not easy because this is a people business. You have to work with and help people in order to have the success that you desire. You are in the people business more so than the product business.

Getting organized may take a little time, however your sponsor will help you. They are there to support you. However, this is your home business and you are responsible for its success. Make time for your business and stay consistent.

Remember:

- ☐ Order your products.
- ☐ Study the Network Marketing business.
- ☐ Learn about your company.
- ☐ Talk to people.
- ☐ Set up presentations.
- ☐ Follow-up.
- ☐ Sponsor, train and assist.
- ☐ Repeat the process.
- ☐ Keep it simple!
- ☐ Have fun!

Training\Personal Development

This subject cannot be over emphasized. Training and Personal Development is a very important part of your success and career in Network Marketing. This is about becoming more knowledgeable about your business, yourself and to better understand people. You will become a better listener, a better speaker and a better presenter. You will also become more professional and gain the confidence needed to explain your business to others. More important, you are learning how to become a leader and expert. The skills that you learn from these trainings will not only help your business but in your personal life as well. This includes work, family, friends and strangers.

If you are new or not-so-new to this industry, your education and training never stops. Everything, everything, everything that you do in your home business is a part of your training. The successes, disappointments and setbacks. It will teach you what to keep doing, what not to do and what you will need to change. There is always more to learn. <u>Leaders who seem to have hit the top fast have a history of trial and errors behind them</u>. What you see is the polished, sharper, wiser version. This should make you excited. Why? Because these individuals were once in your shoes, excited yet confused and unsure.

Have you ever tried to complete a 1000 piece puzzle in an hour or 1 day? You have many scattered pieces that you slowly and patiently attempt to make into a complete picture. Your starting point may be the corner of the puzzle. Someone else may begin in the middle. The goal is to get a complete picture. When starting your Network Marketing business, it is important to understand that like a puzzle, you will get information from many different sources in all shapes and sizes. From books, videos, strangers, your up line, sideline, events, You-Tube, online etc.

This is the information that helps you to become a professional, expert and leader. The information will be scattered and not make sense to you at first. As you continue to plug into training, team calls, company calls, reading and attending local and regional events, everything will begin to take shape and make sense. This information will be your foundation as you grow into a leader. It will shape and sharpen your vision. Your perspective and understanding of this business will come more into focus. It will come together like a puzzle and before you know it, you will have a nearly complete picture. But not yet, because unlike a puzzle, your personal training and development never stops. Always continue to learn and grow as a leader, a professional and a mentor. To your success!

Tips for Success!

1. <u>Write Down Your Goals.</u> Make a list of things that you want to accomplish with this business. Put them where you can see them daily.

2. <u>Learn Your Business.</u> Be able to clearly explain the Network Marketing business model and how it works to your prospects.

3. <u>Prospect or Not</u>? Ask questions to find out if the person is a true prospect. They may not be looking for an opportunity.

4. <u>Have Fun With Your Home Business.</u> This is your business. You have no bosses. Your future is very bright.

5. <u>Take Action</u>! Apply what you have read and studied. Do not become a professional student.

6. <u>Never Quit Your Business!</u> You will face challenges. You will get a few bumps and bruises. You are dealing with people and this is just a part of your growth process and learning curve.

7. <u>Respect Your Home Business.</u> This is not a hustle or

get-rich quick scheme. This is a professional, legitimate business. Treat it as such and let it be reflected in your daily activities, with prospects and team members.

8. <u>Sell the Opportunity of Time Freedom and Financial Freedom</u> to your prospects. This is where the money is. Apple Founder and CEO, Steve Jobs once said, "Sell Dreams not Products".

9. <u>Keep Your Business Simple.</u>

- ☐ Stay qualified by purchasing products each month.
- ☐ Sponsor new reps; build your team.
- ☐ Train and assist your team to do the same.

8. <u>Become a Great Listener</u>. - Ask questions to prospects about what they are looking for. You want to find out IF they are looking for more. It is not about you and your goals, but theirs.

9. <u>Be Honest About Your Business</u>. - Never be ashamed to let everyone know that you have a Network Marketing Home Business. You don't need fancy words or mind games. Tell the truth about what you do, how you do it

and how they can benefit by becoming a part of it.

10. <u>Spend Your Time Wisely</u>. - You time is valuable. Stay focused on things that will help you build a team. If a prospect is not looking for a business opportunity at this time, leave them alone and move on! Work with team members who show you that they are serious and want to do well with their home business.

11. <u>Get Great At Giving Presentations.</u> Watch successful leaders. Practice at home in the mirror or on video. Search on You Tube. There are excellent books available on how to give an effective presentation.

12. <u>Stay Focused</u>! This will be one of your biggest challenges. It is easy to get distracted by outside issues and things that have nothing to do with your business. We all have life challenges, family issues, financial problems, and things that will try to pull you away from your business. Recognize these distractions but, remain focused and committed to your business. Block out the noise, negative voices and dream stealers. Order your products, Build your team. Help others to do the same.

Summary

It is my sincere hope that this information has given you a fresh, new perspective about Network Marketing that will take your great home business to a new level. Move from being an Independent Distributor to the owner of a home business. Network Marketing is a legitimate business model and another way in which companies move their products or services. It is an excellent way to make the kind of money that allows you the real chance to live your goals and dreams like no other business opportunity. This is a simple home business. The key is to first understand the Network Marketing concept and be able to explain it in simple terms to your prospects.

This is a partnership between you, the independent representative and your partner Network Marketing company. Once-a-month, you purchase products from your company. In return, the company pays you (weekly and monthly) when new reps join your team and buy products once-a-month. If you have a burning desire to reach your goals and dreams, your objective is to build a team of reps who will help your company to move as much product as possible. As your team grows, your money grows. Your business is to stay focused, build a team and teach them to do the same. See you at the top!

Terms

☐ <u>Auto Ship</u> – The Network Marketing company will automatically ship products to you each month and charge your credit card or bank account.

☐ <u>Cold Market</u> – People that you do not yet know or have a close relationship with.

☐ <u>Compensation plan</u> – Network Marketing company's payment plan for distributors based on their productivity. Also known as Comp Plan.

☐ <u>Down line</u> – People that you sponsor and others that join your team thru them.

☐ <u>Independent Distributor</u> – The title given when an individual joins a network marketing company. Also known as Representative, Consultant, Rep.)

☐ <u>Network Marketing</u> – A business model based on companies moving their products through a network of independent distributors. Also known as Multi Level Marketing (MLM).

☐ <u>Product Volume</u> – All products are given a volume number based on the size or amount.

☐ Prospect – A potential business partner.

☐ Sponsor – A distributor who is given credit for bringing a new person to join the company and their team.

☐ Time Freedom – The ability to spend your time as you choose.

☐ Up Line – Your sponsor and the team above him/ her. They assist in training you and your team.

☐ Warm Market – People that you know and want to expose to your home business. family members, friends etc.

☐ 1 On 1 – A meeting between you and a prospect.

☐ 2 On 1 – A meeting with you, your support member and a prospect.

☐ 3 way Call – A call with you, your prospect and your support team member. It is designed to let a more experienced person answer questions or invite your prospects to an event.

Suggested Reading and Websites.

These successful leaders and have helped many people reach their goals and dreams financially, in personal growth and leadership. There are others. Below, are some of my favorites:

Books, Web Sites, DVD's and CD's By:

- [ ] Les Brown
- [ ] Dale Carnegie
- [ ] Napoleon Hill
- [ ] John C. Maxwell
- [ ] Jim Rohn
- [ ] Robert Dean Jr. (T.O.P.G.U.N. EXP)
- [ ] Jerry Clark - (www.clubrhino.com)
- [ ] Tony Fleming – www.tonyflemingenterprises.com
- [ ] Brian Beane – www.mentortomillions.com

DEDICATION PAGE

To: Stacy, Shareef, Mark, Pat, Abdul, Abe, Tina and Shirley. The 1st Network Marketing team that I joined. We became like family during our trainings, our travels, our highs and lows. Thank you for your friendship and support!

zuberiwoods@netscape.net